Dean Close Sch
Library

DEAN CLOSE SCHOOL

LIBRARY

This book must be returned by the latest date stamped below.

CANCELLED CANCELLED CANCELLED

The Passages of Joy

by Thom Gunn

Fighting Terms
The Sense of Movement
Poems 1950–1966: A Selection
Positives (*with Ander Gunn*)
Touch
Moly *and* My Sad Captains
Jack Straw's Castle
Selected Poems 1950–1975

THOM GUNN

The Passages of Joy

faber and faber

First published in 1982
by Faber and Faber Limited
3 Queen Square London WC1N 3AU
Printed in Great Britain by
Willmer Brothers Limited, Rock Ferry, Merseyside
All rights reserved

© Thom Gunn, 1982

CONDITIONS OF SALE

This book is sold subject to the conditions that it shall not, by way of
trade or otherwise, be lent, resold, hired out or otherwise circulated
without the publisher's prior consent in any form of binding or cover
other than that in which it is published and without a similar condition
including this condition being imposed on the subsequent purchaser.

British Library Cataloguing in Publication Data

Gunn, Thom
    The passages of joy.
    I. Title
    821'.914   PR6057.U5

    ISBN 0–571–11921–2
    ISBN 0–571–11867–4 Pbk

Contents

One

Elegy

I can almost see it
Thin, tall, half-handsome
the thin hungry sweetness
of his smile gone
as he makes up his mind
and walks behind the barn
in his thin pointed boots
over the crackling eucalyptus leaves
and shoots himself in the head

Even the terror
of leaving life like that
better than the terror
of being unable to handle it

Though I hardly knew him
I rehearse it again and again
Did he smell eucalyptus last?
No it was his own blood
as he choked on it

They keep leaving me
and they don't
tell me they don't
warn me that this is
the last time I'll be seeing them

as they drop away
like Danny or
slowly estrange themselves

There will be no turn of the river
where we are all reunited
in a wonderful party
the picnic spread
all the lost found
as in hide and seek

An odd comfort
that the way we are always
most in agreement
is in playing the same game
where everyone always gets lost

Adultery

Hot beautiful furless animals
played in a clearing opened by their desire
play climaxing to a transparent rage
that raised them above desire itself
—glimpses of clearing after clearing.

Leaving, she recomposed her face
to look as if she had just come
from the new Bergman movie
(which she had in fact seen before).
By the time she was home she'd done it
and her face was all grown over with expression.
Dedicated to her husband, showing
how interesting it had been, how
innovative, a real breakthrough
(you know how I love you, darling?)
he should see it too it would
change his entire outlook.

She played this little drama. And
she half believed it as she shaped it,
having played it before in the interest
of preserving the lovely house,
its rooms airy with freedoms,
the children going to a progressive school,
grass smoked when there were guests,
and philodendrons growing in slow trust.

Her husband looked at her silently,
she seemed, for a moment, an objective matter,
and in his thoughts he reviewed the drama:

[13]

a thicket of good-natured fictions,
not interesting, not
innovative, a real throwback
(you know how bored we are, darling?)
she should see it too it would
change her entire outlook.

Bally *Power Play*

Everybody looks at him playing
the machine hour after hour,
but he hardly raises his gold lashes.
Two fingers move, his hips
lean in almost imperceptibly.
He seldom takes his eyes
from the abstract drama of the ball,
the descent and the reverses
of its brief fortunes. He is
the cool source of all that hurry
and desperate activity, in control,
legs apart, braced arms apart,
seeming alive only at the ends.
His haunches are up against the wood now,
the hard edge which he presses
or which presses him
just where the pelvis begins,
above what in the skeleton
would be no more than a hole.
Bally's drama absorbs him:
amongst the variety and surprise
of the lights, the silver ball
appears, rolls shyly towards him,
meets a wheel of red plastic,
at once bounces away from it,
franticly dashes from side to side
and up and down, it is
trapped, it is released,
it springs to the top again
back to where it entered,
but in the end it must disappear

down the hole at the bottom
—and the fifth act is over
leaving behind it only
the continued inane flickering
of coloured light. Between games
he recognizes me, we chat,
he tells me about broken promises
with a comic-rueful smile
at his need for reassurance,
which is as great as anybody's.
He once told me he never starts
to look for the night's partner
until half an hour before closing time.
The rest is foreplay.

New York

It wasn't ringworm he
explained it was speed
made those blotches all
over his body
                On the catwalk
above the turning wheels, high
on risk
        his luck
and the resources of the body
kept him going we were
balancing
                up there
                        all night
grinning and panting
hands black with machine oil
grease monkeys of risk
and those wheels were turning *fast*

I return to a sixth floor
where I am staying: the sun
ordering the untidy kitchen,
even the terraced black circles
in the worn enamel are bright,
the faucet dripping,
the parakeets chirping quietly
domestic about their cage,
my dear host in the bed and
his Newfoundland on it, together
stretching, half-woken, as
I close the door.

I calm down,
undress, and slip
in between them and think
of household gods.

The Conversation

You pursue the matter
as yet an edgeless
ghost glimpsed
through a tangle of trees

patient in pursuit
all the long conversation,
answers eliciting further
questions, until you
catch up at last and grasp
the matter tenaciously

though it writhe and slither
and change its shape

—it becomes a flame,
but you hold on,
it becomes a stream,
a struggling fish, a heap
of bones, a soap opera,
and you hold on

your talk defines
bit by bit what
it is indeed about, you
grope for the problematical
life of it
        attracted
to the stirrings, the warmth
like a cat to movement
pinpointing, identifying

the pulse of the matter,
so as to shape from
that flickering life
both what is
and what might be

never perfectly defined
never perfect matter
because the words are
fluent, are fluid
replaced, displaced,
overlapping like
currents of flame or water

stopped at last only
by exhaustion or
arbitrary interruption
Good Night, Good
Night, but in
the cold of the night
in the dark bedroom
the elusive matter
floats above your face
like a faint ectoplasm
milky, amoebic, its
wavering existence drawn
from each outbreathing

from the sleeping head

Expression

For several weeks I have been reading
the poetry of my juniors.
Mother doesn't understand,
and they hate Daddy, the noted alcoholic.
They write with black irony
of breakdown, mental institution,
and suicide attempt, of which the experience
does not always seem first-hand.
It is very poetic poetry.

I go to the Art Museum
and find myself looking for something,
though I'm not sure what it is.
I reach it, I recognize it,
seeing it for the first time.
An 'early Italian altar piece'.
The outlined Virgin, her lips
a strangely modern bow of red,
holds a doll-sized Child in her lap.
He has the knowing face of an adult,
and a precocious forelock curling
over the smooth baby forehead. She
is massive and almost symmetrical.
He does not wriggle, nor is he solemn.
The sight quenches, like water
after too much birthday cake.
Solidly there, mother and child
stare outward, two pairs of matching eyes
void of expression.

Selves

I look round the cluttered
icons of your room:
quilt, photo, stuffed bird.
On one wall, the self-portrait
you laboured at these two years
since you broke with your lover.
The new self. It
nags me with its hard eyes,
its simple gaze. Completing it
freed you, apparently,
to other subjects, for
a dozen new sketches are tacked
on another wall. A nude
lolls on some cushions;
a winding road seen from above
pierces the countryside
with a big S.
                    I do miss
what you formerly were,
the vulnerable and tender man
I have dreamed about
three nights running. I suppose
it was an imaginary son
that I held onto during this time
of mess and misunderstanding.
But sons grow up,
imaginary ones as well,
and perpetual children are tedious.
Day after day you
went to the gym
where you lifted toward nothing

and your body kept pace
with the body in the self-portrait
you were painting. You lifted
barbells to lower them, but
at the same time you were learning
to carry the other,
the constant weight, the weight
it is necessary to carry.
You got used to the feel
like a hitchhiker
shifting his knapsack
as he improvises his route
along roads already adjusted
to their terrain. Here in your sketch
the roadway pushes forward
like a glittering unsheathed serpent
that tests with the flicker
of his tongue from
side to side as he advances.
You dare place it in the exact
centre of the page from where
it twists upward with
the strength of its pliancy.
It adapts to the rigid
rocky folds of the mountain's skirt
and the soft slopes of the coast
that it slips between
—agile and tactful!—
sometimes lost in a bend
but coming round again:
a flexile sinewy unchecked
curving line it
narrows into the distance where
it steals at last
right off the top of the paper.

A Waking Dream

They are massing at the bank
on the slippery mud, the only light
leaking from the world behind them.
In the middle of the crowd
not in the front pushing but not laggard
on his way to the grey river,
one figure catches my eye.
I see in a strong glint of light
a thick neck half curtained
by black hair, and the back of a head
that I dare recognize,
though knowing it could be another's.
Fearfully, 'Tony!' I call.
And the head turns: it is indeed his,
but he looks through me and beyond me,
he cannot see who spoke,
he is working out a different fate.

Sweet Things

He licks the last chocolate ice cream
from the scabbed corners of his mouth.
Sitting in the sun on a step
outside the laundromat,
mongoloid Don turns his crewcut head
and spies me coming down the street.
'Hi!' He says it with the mannered
enthusiasm of a fraternity brother.
'Take me cross the street!?' part
question part command. I hold
the sticky bunch of small fingers in mine
and we stumble across. They sell
peaches and pears over there,
the juice will dribble down your chin.
He turns before I leave him,
saying abruptly with the same
mixture of order and request
'Gimme a quarter!?' I
don't give it, never have, not to him,
I wonder why not, and as I
walk on alone I realize
it's because his seven-year-old mind
never recognizes me, me
for myself, he only says hi
for what he can get, quarters to
buy sweet things, one after another,
he goes from store to store, from
candy store to ice cream store to
bakery to produce market, unending
quest for the palate's pleasure. Then

out to panhandle again,
more quarters, more sweet things.

My errands are toothpaste,
vitamin pills and a book of stamps.
No self-indulgence there.
But who's this coming up? It's
John, no Chuck, how
could his name have slipped my mind.
Chuck gives a one-sided smile, he stands
as if fresh from a laundromat,
a scrubbed cowboy, Tom Sawyer
grown up, yet stylish, perhaps
even careful, his dark hair
slicked back in the latest manner.
When he shakes my hand I feel
a dry finger playfully bending inward
and touching my palm in secret.
'It's a long time
since we got together,' says John.
Chuck, that is. The warm teasing
tickle in the cave of our handshake
took my mind off toothpaste,
snatched it off, indeed.
How handsome he is in
his lust and energy, in his
fine display of impulse.
Boldly 'How about now?' I say
knowing the answer. My boy
I could eat you whole. In the long pause
I gaze at him up and down and
from his blue sneakers back to the redawning
one-sided smile. We know our charm.
We know delay makes pleasure great.
In our eyes, on our tongues,

we savour the approaching delight
of things we know yet are fresh always.
Sweet things. Sweet things.

The Cat and the Wind

A small wind
blows across the hedge
into the yard.
The cat cocks her ears
—multitudinous rustling
and crackling all around—
her pupils dwindle
to specks in
her yellow eyes
that stare first upward
and then on every side
unable to single out
any one thing
to pounce on,
for all together
as if orchestrated,
twigs, leaves,
small pebbles, pause
and start and pause
in their shifting,
their rubbing
against each other.

She is still listening
when the wind is already
three gardens off.

Small Plane in Kansas

C'mon said the pilot and
the three of us climbed onto
the wing and into the snug plane.
With a short run we took off,
lurched upward, soared,
changed direction, missed a treetop,
and found an altitude.
Silo and wood below us
perfect toys, the field
so close you could see
the nested half-circles
where the tractor had turned in ploughing.

That's how it is in the flying dream,
where I step into a wind
with the seven-league boots of euphoria,
letting go, rising, each
pulse a step. Out there
from the height of self-love
I survey the reduced world.

Mastered by mastering,
I so much belong to the wind
I become of it, a gust
that flows, mindless for ever
along unmarked channel
and wall-less corridor where
the world's invisible currents run,
like symptoms, like remedies.

The Exercise

O uncontrollable . . .

Sad little lake, your
glittering grey and the muted
green of overhanging bough
are fresh in memory as
the soft paralysis that had grown in me.
The wider that adolescent
uncertainty of everything,
the sharper was the beauty of
that horrible little lake
within a wood within a fence
put up by the Surrey commuters.

But when wind took over!
On the shore I became of it,
braced and full, or
it partook of me.
It was like an impulse of freedom,
thing but no thing,
here and nowhere,
known only by result, where
for example it pressed water,
blew back trees on the shore,
or combed the long grasses.
I straightened up, facing it,
it seemed a kind of certainty
that I took into me with each breath.
The boisterous presence rummaged
at large in the wood, without it
the trees would have lacked
a condition of their growth.
This bough was blown one way

day by day, month by month,
until that was the way it grew,
but springy and tough
from bearing against wind
to stay upright at all.

Though the wind was like
impulse, it was not impulse.
If I was formed by it, I was formed
by the exercise it gave me.
Exercise in stance, and
in the muscle of feeling.
I became robust standing against it,
as I breathed it so gladly.
The trees resisted, stood, and
gradually bent. The deep grass
accepted, bending at once.
I walked from the lake through
the glum shine of the suburban wood.
The wind blew against me till
I tingled with knowledge.
The swiftly changing
played upon the slowly changing.

Hide and Seek

Children play on into
the summer evening, the block
full of excited shouts.
These girls tied a rope
to the lamp post   higher and higher.
Others sing slightly off-key
counting-out songs, and songs
from TV and Sunday school.
Across the street
                    boys and girls
whoosh by on skate boards
that rumble to the end of the block.

From trees behind the houses
birds are calling
about the gathering night.
Chicks scramble
among the familiar ordure
loose-clotted in the nest.

In their fathers' gardens
children are hiding
up in orchard trees, seeking
to be lost and found.

Mother comes down
for the youngest
and as the dark thickens
for the oldest too.

Indoors, under a naked bulb,
eight puppies sleep
close against the huge hairy body
of their mother. The bees
have returned to their Queen.
The crescent moon rises
nine-tenths of it still hidden
but imperceptibly moving
below the moving stars
and hugging the earth.

As Expected

Most of his friends, as expected,
went into service. Two
became pilots, swooping over
lush Vietnamese lowland in their bombers,
high on the orgasmic shriek
of Led Zeppelin over the intercom.

Larry chose a slower route.

He was assigned a grubby
roomful of young men sitting around
idle, or idle on their cots.
One who had been high-spirited
earlier, lay in deep sleep
knocked out by thorazine all day.
Their hair was cropped. Some
would have to be hosed down.
Burdens-on-society.

They looked like ninepins.
But he found that none had head-lice
and let them grow their hair.
They started to look
as if they had different names.

A whole night he watched them
till they forgot he was there.
They paid neighbourly visits
bed to bed. One of them
had composed a little tune
made up of three sounds.

One had invented a game
for the fingers of both hands.
Larry watched:
                if the unteachable
can teach themselves, it follows
they can be taught by others.

One learned to eat without help.
One learned toilet training
for the first time in his nineteen years.

When he came on his shift
they shambled up, poorly co-ordinated,
wild-eyed, and with faces uncomposed.
'Larry! Larry!' they cried out,
they giggled and embraced him,
stumbling like kittens, inarticulate
like tulips bending in a wet wind,
and learning as they went, like humans.

When the testing time was over,
Larry and the pilots went to college.
The young men in the other institution
were given to other keepers: and they were
retarded, unteachable,
                as expected.

The Menace

an opposition lurks
in the hollows of the cranium, hides
in the next white chamber
of the linked caverns
haunts the brain hunts the sleeper
through stifling passages

guard   father
executioner   angel of death
delivering doctor   judge
cop   castrator

the-one-who-wants-to-get-me

Come out, come out, wherever you are,
come on out of your hiding place,
put on a body, show me a face.

. .   . .   . .

So, to objectify.
                He congeals
from what had seemed sheets
of fallen rainwater
on the pavement between stores.

He leaps from the night
fully armed, a djinn
of human stature.

In the flash of his leap
his helmet and sunshades
seem to reflect everything,
to send it back on itself
untouched and unseen.
Both hands hang heavy
gloved for obscure purpose.
There is menace, perhaps cruelty,
in his inert mouth, suggesting,
as it does, merely the latent.

But I stand against him,
and he settles reluctantly
into a perturbed gleam.
Suddenly, by passing headlights,
I can see what he was, clothed
mannequin in a store window.

I am, am I,
the-one-who-wants-to-get-me

.   .   . .   . .

The quick air of a new street
hits my face, mixed smell
of the meat district—
cobbles and flags thick
with accumulated grease
from slaughtered animals,
almost the sweet smell of a dairy
when the milk is brought in
in pails, to be strained.

Romantics in leather bars
watch the play of light and dark

on the shine of worn wood,
bottles and badboy uniforms,

frame fantasies like the beginnings
of sentences, form opening clauses,
seeking a plausible conjunction
that a sentence can turn on
to compound the daydream.

. .   . .   . .

In a theatre of reflection
I encounter again
the exemplary figure,
now can see into
the gleam. Eyes
move behind it,
the mouth smiles, the talk
though sparing suggests
an unceasing thick
traffic of feeling.

He is not a real soldier
but a soldier
inducted by himself
into an army of fantasy
and he greets another.

This time the glitter
pulls me after it.
In a little room
we play at large
with the dull idea of the male
strenuous in his limitations.
We play without deceit,

compressing symbol into fetish,
which is as it were
an object vivified
from inside, a lamp
that abruptly wakens desire
in the night,
            we play
with light and dark.

.   .   . .   . .

From imagination's forcing-house
my man produces
surprise after surprise:

the life of meat,
the charm of institutions,
the banquet of milk.

The finest palate feels
moments before tasting it
the charge of semen,
and only afterwards greets
the sweet and salt in one.

. .   . .   . .

Gregory Bateson watching dogs at play: 'The playful nip
denotes the bite, but it does not denote what would be
denoted by the bite.'

'But' is the word that introduces the second, opposing
statement into this sentence. It is a conjunction that changes
the simple sentence of the first clause into a compound one.
The opposition it introduces does not contradict or delete
what came before; instead, the whole sentence could be said

to turn on it, since it qualifies and extends the meaning of
the first clause, which would otherwise be incomplete.

. .   . .   . .

I picture a drawing room
where a broad-shouldered man
in an evening gown
who outJudys Judy
conquers by parody
the idea of the female
the frivolous bitch in his head
who haunts him and compels him.
By sullying her poise
by inhabiting it
with his desires
and compounding intentions
he partly exorcises
partly possesses her.

. .   . .   . .

I think it must be
getting light, a sly
gleam touches a shirt
thrown over a chair,
a wind from the river
nips my cheek.

If we have fought
across the fields of absurdity
we have through our cunning
fought a real army whose
perfected barracks are houses
for the beaten and the dulled.

And we sleep at the end
as a couple. I cup
the fine warm back,
broad fleshed shoulder blades.
We gave the menace
our bodies: his arms
were our arms,
his sperm ours.
His terror became
our play.

. .   . .   . .

Silt settles: windows clear.
The great piers are being searched
by the wind, but their secrets hide
deep in the meshed gleam of the river.

The 'exemplary figure'
strides away, i.e.
a cheerful man in workclothes
stumbles off grinning
'Bye babe gotta get to the job.'

I see as he goes
how admirably the loose
or withholding stuff of his clothing
has adapted to his body, revealing
what he has become.

the-one-who-wants-to-get-me

guard   angel
guardian   delivering

Two

Song of a Camera

for Robert Mapplethorpe

I cut the sentence
out of a life
out of the story
with my little knife

Each bit I cut
shows one alone
dressed or undressed
young full-grown

Look at the bits
He eats he cries
Look at the way
he stands he dies

so that another
seeing the bits
and seeing how
none of them fits

wants to add
adverbs to verbs
A bit on its own
simply disturbs

Wants to say
as well as see
wants to say
valiantly

[45]

interpreting
some look in the eyes
a triumph mixed up
with surprise

I cut this sentence
look again
for cowardice
boredom pain

Find what you seek
find what you fear
and be assured
nothing is here

I am the eye
that cut the life
you stand you lie
I am the knife

Waitress

At one they hurry in to eat.
Loosed from the office job they sit
But somehow emptied out by it
And eager to fill up with meat.
   Salisbury Steak with Garden Peas.

The boss who orders them about
Lunches elsewhere and they are free
To take a turn at ordering me.
I watch them hot and heavy shout:
   Waitress I want the Special please.

My little breasts, my face, my hips,
My legs they study while they feed
Are not found on the list they read
While wiping gravy off their lips.
   Here Honey gimme one more scoop.

I dream that while they belch and munch
And talk of Pussy, Ass, and Tits,
And sweat into their double knits,
I serve them up their Special Lunch:
   Bone Hash, Grease Pie, and Leather Soup.

Keats at Highgate

A cheerful youth joined Coleridge on his walk
('Loose,' noted Coleridge, 'slack, and not well-dressed')
Listening respectfully to the talk talk talk
Of First and Second Consciousness, then pressed
The famous hand with warmth and sauntered back
Homeward in his own state of less dispersed
More passive consciousness—passive, not slack,
Whether of Secondary type or First.

He made his way toward Hampstead so alert
He hardly passed the small grey ponds below
Or watched a sparrow pecking in the dirt
Without some insight swelling the mind's flow
That banks made swift. Everything put to use.
Perhaps not well-dressed but oh no not loose.

His Rooms in College

All through the damp morning he works, he reads.
The papers of his students are interrupted
Still by the raw fury, the awkward sadness
His marriage has become. The young serious voices
Are drowned by her remembered piteous wail
'Discovering' the one unfaithfulness
He never did commit.
                              Be more specific.
What do they have ahead of them, poor dears,
This kind of thing?
                              Today no supervisions;
But though he meant these hours for his research
He takes a book, not even in his 'field',
And some note touches him, he goes on reading
Hours long into the afternoon from which
The same low river fog has never lifted.
If every now and then he raises his eyes
And stares at winter lawns below, each time
He sees their hard blurred slopes the less. He reads,
He reads, until the chapel clock strikes five,
And suddenly discovers that the book,
Unevenly, gradually, and with difficulty,
Has all along been showing him its mind
(Like no one ever met at a dinner party),
And his attention has become prolonged
To the quiet passion with which he in return
Has given himself completely to the book.
He looks out at the darkened lawns, surprised
Less by the loss of grief than by the trust.

June

In these two separate rooms we sit,
I at my work, you at yours.
I am at once buried in it
And sensible of all outdoors.

The month is cool, as if on guard,
High fog holds back the sky for days,
But in their sullen patch of yard
The Oriental Poppies blaze.

Separate in the same weather
The parcelled buds crack pink and red,
And rise from different plants together
To shed their bud-sheaths on the bed,

And stretch their crumpled petals free,
That nurse the box of hardening seed,
In the same hour, as if to agree
On what could not have been agreed.

Another All Night Party

Another all night party over.
Another night of passages,
Stairs, and angelic messages.
Each cupboard in the back led through
To where the style of dance was new.
One there was rumoured with his lover.

The basement sunk beneath it all
Was watered by a living stream,
As from a grand prophetic dream,
The puddles candling in reflection.
Startled, I almost lost direction
In that wet purgatorial hall.

The drugs wear off, my friend and I
Head for the sidewalks of the day.
Fifth Street at 7 a.m. in May.
So this is where the night-stream led:
Pavements as empty as my head,
Stone city under pale blue sky.

Whereas the night was charged and dense
Now spire and tower piece out the blue.
We laugh, and once more we've run through
Historic night to simpler dawn.
Though even the street we walk upon
Might sparkle with a difference.

I stretch, almost too tired to think,
Cool as a hand freed from a glove

Dean Close School Library

That it began to feel part of,
It had been on so long. We greet
Two other guests on Market Street
And hit the Balcony for a drink.

San Francisco Streets

I've had my eye on you
   For some time now.
You're getting by it seems,
   Not quite sure how.
But as you go along
   You're finding out
What different city streets
   Are all about.

Peach country was your home.
   When you went picking
You ended every day
   With peach fuzz sticking
All over face and arms,
   Intimate, gross,
Itching like family,
   And far too close.

But when you came to town
   And when you first
Hung out on Market Street
   That was the worst:
Tough little group of boys
   Outside Flagg's Shoes.
You learned to keep your cash.
   You got tattoos.

Then by degrees you rose
   Like country cream—
Hustler to towel boy,
   Bath house and steam;

Tried being kept a while—
    But felt confined,
One brass bed driving you
    Out of your mind.

Later on Castro Street
    You got new work
Selling chic jewelry.
    And as sales clerk
You have at last attained
    To middle class.
(No one on Castro Street
    Peddles his ass.)

You gaze out from the store.
    Watching you watch
All the men strolling by
    I think I catch
Half-veiled uncertainty
    In your expression.
Good looks and great physiques
    Pass in procession.

You've risen up this high—
    How, you're not sure.
Better remember what
    Makes you secure.
Fuzz is still on the peach,
    Peach on the stem.
Your looks looked after you.
    Look after them.

The Miracle

'Right to the end, that man, he was so hot
That driving to the airport we stopped off
At some MacDonald's and do you know what,
We did it there. He couldn't get enough.'
—'There at the counter?'—'No, that's public stuff:

'There in the rest room. He pulled down my fly,
And through his shirt I felt him warm and trim.
I squeezed his nipples and began to cry
At losing this, my miracle, so slim
That I could grip my wrist in back of him.

'Then suddenly he dropped down on one knee
Right by the urinal in his only suit
And let it fly, saying Keep it there for me,
And smiling up. I can still see him shoot.
Look at that snail-track on the toe of my boot.'

—'Snail-track?'—'Yes, there.'—'That was six months ago.
How can it still be there?'—'My friend, at night
I make it shine again, I love him so,
Like they renew a saint's blood out of sight.
But we're not Catholic, see, so it's all right.'

The Victim

Oh dead punk lady with the knack
Of looking fierce in pins and black,
The suburbs wouldn't want you back.

You wished upon a shooting star
And trusted in your wish as far
As he was famous and bizarre.

The band broke up, its gesture made.
And though the music stopped, you stayed.
Now it was with sharp things he played:

Needles and you, not with the band,
Till something greater than you planned
Opened erect within his hand.

You smiled. He pushed it through your shirt
Deep in your belly, where it hurt.
You turned, and ate the carpet's dirt.

And then not understanding why
He watched out with a heavy eye
The several hours you took to die.

The news was full of his fresh fame.
He O.D.'d, ending up the same.
Poor girl, poor girl, what was your name?

Three

Painkillers

The King of rock 'n roll
grown pudgy, almost matronly,
Fatty in gold lamé,
mad King encircled
by a court of guards, suffering
delusions about assassination,
obsessed by guns, fearing
rivalry and revolt

popping his skin
with massive hits of painkiller

dying at 42.

What was the pain?
Pain had been the colours
of the bad boy with the sneer.

The story of pain, of separation,
was the divine comedy
he had translated
from black into white.

For white children too
the act of naming the pain
unsheathed
a keen joy at the heart of it.

Here they are still!
the disobedient
who keep a culture alive

by subverting it, turning
for example a subway
into a garden of graffiti.

But the puffy King
lived on, his painkillers
neutralizing, neutralizing,
until he became
ludicrous in performance.

The enthroned cannot revolt.
What was the pain
he needed to kill
if not the ultimate pain

of feeling no pain?

Slow Waker

I look at the cousin,
eighteen, across the breakfast.
He had to be called and called.
He smiles, but without
conviction. He will not
have tea, oh OK,
if it's no trouble,
he will have tea.

His adult face is brand-new.
Once the newness
clears up and it has got
an expression or two
besides bewilderment
he could be a handsome
devil. He could be
a carpenter, a poet, it's
all possible . . .
impossible. The future
is not a word in his mouth.

That, for him, is the trouble:
he lay in bed caught deep
in the mire between
sleep and awake, neither
alert nor resting,
between the flow of night,
ceaselessly braiding itself,
and the gravelly beach
that our soles have thickened on.

Nobody has ever told him
he is goodlooking,
just that his feet smell.

He paces through alien London
all day. Everything
is important and unimportant.
He feeds only by osmosis.
He stares at the glint
and blunt thrust of traffic. He
wants to withdraw.

He wants to withdraw into
a small space, like
the cupboard under the stairs
where the vacuum cleaner is kept,
so he can wait, and doze,
and get in nobody's way.

The Girls Next Door

Laughter of sisters, mingling,
separating, but so alike you
sometimes couldn't tell
which was which,
as in a part-song.
I could hear them from outdoors
over the wall
that separated two gardens,
where the lilac bush on our side
was tattered by the passage
of domestic cats, on their constant
wary patrol through
systems of foliage. And then
late afternoons, the sound
of scales on the piano,
of rudimentary tunes.
Evenings, one of them
would call their cat in,
'poor wandering one', a joke
out of Gilbert and Sullivan.
                              And again
laughter, two voices
like two hands on a piano,
separate but not at variance,
practice in a sunlit room.

Today, many years later,
the younger of the two
tells me about her divorce.
On the phone last week he said
'I didn't give you

the house for ever,
you know. You could learn
a trade at night school.'
'But,' she exclaims to me,
'I'm 49!'

An hour later, from the next room,
I hear her with one of her sons,
and suddenly her laughter
breaks out, as it used to.
Though she is on her own
—for the other sister
died long ago, in her teens—
it is unchanged, a sweet
high stumble of the voice,
rudimentary tune.

Donahue's Sister

She comes level with him at
the head of the stairs
with a slight, arrogant smile
and an inward look, muttering
some injunction to her private world.
Drunk for four days now.

He's unable to get through.
She's not there to get through to.
When he does get through,
next week, it will all sound
exaggerated. She will apologize as if
all too humanly she has caused him
a minute inconvenience.

That sudden tirade last night,
such conviction and logic
—had she always hated him or
was it the zombie speaking?

Scotch for breakfast,
beer all morning.
Fuelling her private world, in which
she builds her case against the public.
Catching at ends of phrases
in themselves meaningless,
as if to demonstrate how well
she keeps abreast.
            A zombie,
inaccessible and sodden replacement.

He glances at her, her
body stands light and meatless,
and estimates how high he would have
to lift it to launch it
into a perfect trajectory over
the narrow dark staircase
so that it would land on its head
on the apartment-house mosaic of the hallway
and its skull would break in two
—an eggshell full of alcohol—
leaving, at last, his sister
lying like the garbage by the front door
in a pool of Scotch and beer,
understandably, this time, inaccessible.

At an Intersection

I couldn't take my eyes off
the old woman ranging around,
cursing at random,
she was tethered to crisis
like a mobbed witch:

yes, she looked like that,
like an old peasant witch
out of place anywhere,
even at the intersection
where worldly Market Street
meets the slum of Sixth
—head tied up in a kerchief,
apple cheeks, and long nose
as bright and sharp as Anger.

She was screaming abuse
at two plump young cops
who drove off chuckling
in their upholstered police car.
Rambling she cast about
after objects for her rage.
At the bus stop she came against
a young bearded face: it
fixed her with a long pitying look,
which fed her, which fed her.
She discovered an empty pop-bottle,
she danced in front of the traffic
stopped at the red light, waving it,
and smashed it on the asphalt.

Everyone watched, either laughing
or in silent dismay as she flung
her seventy-year-old body about
with the strength of a baby just weaned.

Another time, in his room,
a certain man said to me,
'Please don't be upset
by what I am going to do.
It has nothing to do with you.'
And where he lay he pulled
a pillow over his face
and roared into it several times
—long muffled belches of rage—
as if his trouble was
a sudden cramp or attack
of indigestion to be got rid of
sensibly, by learned measures,

as if it could be
absorbed in the neutral stuff
of a pillow, or by bystanders
who turn away, laughing,

as if the causes
could be smothered with the cry,
but the causes are forgotten
and the cry returns,

                         out of control,

raging about an intersection
where the red light is jammed
and the traffic stopped,

the drivers gazing in discomfort
at an anger
unspent, unspendable.

A Drive to Los Alamos

Past mesas in yellow ruin,
breaking up like everything,

upward to the wide plateau
where the novelist went to school,
at the Ranch School for Boys,
in 1929. And that was
all there had been up there.

(His face 'borrowed flesh',
his imagination disguised
in an implacable suit.)
Somebody asked: were you
considered a sissy?
No, he said
in his quiet voice, I was neither
popular nor unpopular.

(The twenty-five boys
of that expensive spartan school
laconic on horses
hunted among the burnt-out furnaces
of the wildness. Where
the rock fell it stayed.)

One building remained, massive
and made of good brown wood,
surrounded now by shoddy
prefab suburb—a street
named after Oppenheimer,
another Trinity Drive.

In the Science Museum
we looked through a brochure
for the extinct school.
That was Mr. So-and-so, he said.
That was the infirmary, that was
where the lucky boys went.
(Aware, quietly, of what the past
becomes, golden in ruin.)
Those were the sleeping porches.
Yes, they were cold.
Another picture showed a healthy boy
after a hunt, with the dead deer.
That was Jack Matthews.
(I make up the name,
since I do not remember it,
but he did.)

Transients and Residents

a sequence interrupted

'Albert Hotel,
    Transients and Residents'
                —New York, 1970
'Time hovers o'er, impatient to destroy,
And shuts up all the Passages of Joy.'
                —Samuel Johnson,
                    'The Vanity of Human Wishes'

Falstaff

I always hope to find you circling here
Round the bar's table, playing your old game,
In one hand pool cue, in the other beer.
Vast in your foul burnoose, you'd be the same:
Bullying your little entourage of boys
—Goodlooking but untrustworthy—and later
Ordering them home where, turning up the noise,
You'd party through the night. Neighbourhood satyr,
Old friend, for years you bullied all of us
And did so, you were sure, for our own good.
You took no notice if we made a fuss
Or didn't enjoy ourselves the way we should.
I think of one place you were living at
And all the parties that you used to throw
(That must be when you wore a feathered hat,
Several burnooses, so to speak, ago);
You cooked each evening for some twenty heads,
Not just for streetboys then, for everyone
Who came in want of food or drugs or beds.
The bonus was your boisterous sense of fun.

[72]

And though as years have passed your bullying love
Became more desperate (sometimes indeed
Stripped by a ruthlessness you weren't above
It showed itself more nakedly as need);
And though the parties that you gave took place
In other people's houses now, until
They kicked you out for taking all the space;
And though the drugs themselves got questionable—
Too many evenings in the bar have passed

Full of mere chatter and the pumping sound
Of disco on the juke box since you last
Roared down it for next player or next round.

If you are sick—that's what they say in here
Almost as if by way of an excuse—
The cancer must have rendered you, my dear,
Damnably thin beneath the foul burnoose.

Crystal

He arrives, and makes deliveries, after 3:00,
Then strolls to a ramp that leads up from the dance,
And sits apart, quiet, hands clasped round a knee,
Smelling the fresh-sawed planks, no doubt. Not tense—
Fixed, merely. While he watches us, his face
Is almost readable, his recessed shape
Gleams like a friendly visitor's from space.
As in a sense it is, now. To escape
The sheer impurity of the other lives,
He has always been extreme, he puts his soul
Into each role in turn, where he survives
Till it is incarnation more than role.
Now it is Dealer. 52, tall, scarred,
His looks get nobler every year, I find,
Almost heroic.
           I once saw in the yard
A half-grown foxglove that he brings to mind
Here, so magnificently self-enwrapped.
Its outer leaves were toothed and all alike.
With a rough symmetry they overlapped
Circling around the budded central spike,
Still green. Dense with its destiny, it waited
Till it might fling itself up into flower.

Now he sits similarly concentrated,
And edged, and similarly charged with power,
Certain of that potential, which his mood
Fairly feeds on, but which is still contained.

The foxglove flowers in its damp solitude
Before its energy fades, and in the end

The chemical in the man will fade as well.
Meanwhile he watches how the dancing feet
Move to the rhythms of the fresh wood-smell;
Inside the crowded night he feels complete.

Crosswords

Your cup of instant coffee by the bed
Cold as the Sixties . . . and you chat with me.
For days your excellent strict mind has fed
Only on crossword puzzles and TV.
Though the least self-indulgent man I know
You lie propped up here like an invalid
Pursuing your recuperation, slow,
Relentless, from the world you used to need.
You have seen reason to remove your ground
Far from the great circle where you toiled,
Where they still call their wares and mill around
Body to body, unpausing and unspoiled.
You smell of last week. You do not move much.
You lay your things beside you on the bed
In a precarious pile one sudden touch
Would bring down on you: letters read and reread,
Pens, opera programmes, cigarettes and books.
I think you disturb nothing but the mind.
There: I catch one of those familiar looks
Of thinking through. You reach, you almost find.
Beneath a half-frown your eyes concentrate,
Focussed on what you saw or dreamt you saw,
Alight with their attentiveness, and wait.
Yes, you are active still, you can't withdraw.

Now we take up again the much-discussed
The never-settled topics, a) change, b)
Limits of judgment, and of course c) trust.
We talk, explore, agree and disagree.
. . . I think that you just put me in the wrong.
You want to win, old jesuit. So do I.

You never liked it easy for too long.
I once found that this bed on which you lie
Is just a blanket-covered length of board.
For you, hardness authenticates, and when
Things get too easy, well you make them hard.
. . . We compromise. Then off we go again,
On our renewed cross-country walking tour,
Off with a swinging stride uphill. Stop, though,
Before there's time to disagree once more.
I want to tell you what you no doubt know:

How glad I am to be back at your school
Where it's through contradictions that I learn.
Obsessive and detached, ardent and cool,
You make me think of rock thrown free to turn
At the globe's side, both with and not with us,
Keeping yourself in a companionable
Chilled orbit by the simultaneous
Repulsion and attraction to it all.

Interruption

Though ready in my chair I do not write.
The desk lamp crook'd above me where I lean
Describes a circle round me with its light
—Singling me out; the room falls back unseen.
So, my own island. I can hear the rain
Coming on stealthily, and the rustle grows
Into a thin taptapping on the pane
I stare against, where my reflection glows.

Beyond by day shows that damp square of earth
On which I act out my experiments
—Sowing a seed and watching for the birth:
A tiny pair of leaves, pale rudiments
That might in time grow stronger to assume
A species' characteristics, till I see
Each fresh division soaring into bloom,
Beauty untouched by personality.

My mind shifts inward from such images.
What am I after—and what makes me think
The group of poems I have entered is
Interconnected by a closer link
Than any snapshot album's?
                                           I can try
At least to get my snapshots accurate.
(The thought that I take others' pictures, I,
Far too conceited to find adequate
Pictures they take of me!) Starting outside,
You save yourself some time while working in:
Thus by the seen the unseen is implied.
I like loud music, bars, and boisterous men.

You may from this conclude I like the things
That help me if not lose then leave behind,
What else, the self.
                         I trust the seedling wings,
Yet taking off on them I leave to find.

I find what? In the letters that I send
I imitate unconsciously the style
Of the recipients: mimicking each friend,
I answer expectations, and meanwhile
Can analyse, or drawl a page of wit,
And range, depending on the friend addressed,
From literary to barely literate.
I manage my mere voice on postcards best.

My garden is the plants that I have got
By luck, skill, purchase, robbery, or gift.
From foxglove, lily, pink, and bergamot
I raise leafed unity, a blossoming drift
Where I once found weed waiting out a drought.
But this side of the glass, dry as at noon,
I see the features that my lamp picks out—
Colourless, unjoined, like a damaged moon.

Talbot Road

where I lived in London 1964–5

1

Between the pastel boutiques
of Notting Hill and the less defined
windier reaches of the Harrow Road,
all blackened brick, was the street
built for burghers, another Belgravia,
but eventually fallen
to labourers ('No Coloured or Irish
Need Apply') and then like the veins
of the true-born Englishman
filling with a promiscuous mix:
Pole, Italian, Irish, Jamaican,
rich jostling flow. A Yugoslav restaurant
framed photographs of exiled princes,
but the children chattered with a London accent.
I lived on Talbot Road
for a year. The excellent room
where I slept, ate, read, and wrote,
had a high ceiling, on the borders
stucco roses were painted blue.
You could step through the window
to a heavy balcony and even
(unless the drain was blocked)
sup there on hot evenings.
That's what I call complete access—
to air, to street, to friendship:
for, from it, I could see, blocks away,
the window where Tony, my old friend,

toiled at translation. I too tried
to render obscure passages into clear English,
as I try now.

2

Glamorous and difficult friend,
helper and ally. As students
enwrapt by our own romanticism,
innocent poet and actor we had posed
we had played out parts to each other
I have sometimes thought
like studs in a whorehouse.
—But he had to deal
with the best looks of his year.
If 'the rich are different from us',
so are the handsome. What
did he really want? Ah that question . . .

Two romances going on in London,
one in Northampton, one in Ireland,
probably others. Friends and lovers
all had their own versions of him.
Fantastical duke of dark corners,
he never needed to lie:
you had learned not to ask questions.

The fire of his good looks.
But almost concealed by the fringe of fire,
behind the mighty giving of self,
at the centre of the jollity, there was
something withheld, slow, something—
what? what? A damp smoulder of discontent.
He would speculate about 'human relations'
which we were supposed to view

—*vide* Forster, *passim,* etc.—
as an end, a good in themselves.
He did not find them so.

Finally it came to this,
the poses had come undone so far:
he loved you more for your faults
than for anything you could give him.
When once in a pub I lost my temper,
I shouldered my way back from the urinal
and snapped, 'I was too angry to piss.'
The next day he exclaimed with delight,
'Do you know that was the first time
you have ever been angry with me?'
As some people wait for a sign of love,
he had waited how many years
for a sign of anger,
for a sign of other than love.

3

A London returned to after twelve years.
On a long passage between two streets
I met my past self lingering there
or so he seemed
a youth of about nineteen glaring at me
from a turn of desire. He held his look
as if shielding it from wind.
Our eyes parleyed, then we touched
in the conversation of bodies.
Standing together on asphalt openly,
we gradually loosened into a shared laughter.
This was the year, the year of reconciliation
to whatever it was I had come from,
the prickly heat of adolescent emotion,
premature staleness and self-contempt.
In my hilarity, in my luck,
I forgave myself for having had a youth.

I started to heap up pardons
even in anticipation. On Hampstead Heath
I knew every sudden path from childhood,
the crooks of every climbable tree.
And now I engaged these at night,
and where I had played hide and seek
with neighbour children, played as an adult
with troops of men whose rounds intersected
at the Orgy Tree or in the wood
of birch trunks gleaming like mute watchers
or in tents of branch and bush

surrounded by the familiar smell
of young leaf—salty, explosive.
In a Forest of Arden, in a summer night's dream
I forgave everybody his teens.

4

But I came back, after the last bus,
from Hampstead, Wimbledon, the pubs,
the railway arches of the East End,
I came back to Talbot Road,
to the brick, the cement Arthurian faces,
the area railings by coal holes,
the fat pillars of the entrances.
My balcony filled up with wet snow.
When it dried out Tony and I
would lunch there in the sunshine
on veal-and-ham pie, beer, and salad.
I told him about my adventures.
He wondered aloud if he would be happier
if he were queer like me.
How could he want, I wondered,
to be anything but himself?
Then he would have to be off,
off with his jaunty walk,
where, I didn't ask or guess.

At the end of my year, before I left,
he held a great party for me
on a canal boat. The party slipped
through the watery network of London,
grid that had always been glimpsed
out of the corner of the eye
behind fences or from the tops of buses.
Now here we were, buoyant on it,

picnicking, gazing in mid-mouthful
at the backs of buildings, at smoke-black walls
coral in the light of the long evening,
at what we had suspected all along
when we crossed the bridges we now passed under,
gliding through the open secret.

5

That was fifteen years ago.
Tony is dead, the block where I lived
has been torn down. The mind
is an impermanent place, isn't it,
but it looks to permanence.
The street has opened and opened up
into no character at all. Last night
I dreamt of it as it might have been,
the pavement by the church railings
was wet with spring rain,
it was night, the streetlamps' light
rendered it into an exquisite etching.
Sentimental postcard of a dream,
of a moment between race-riots!

But I do clearly remember my last week,
when every detail brightened with meaning.
A boy was staying with (I would think)
his grandmother in the house opposite.
He was in his teens, from the country perhaps.
Every evening of that week
he sat in his white shirt at the window
—a Gothic arch of reduced proportion—
leaning on his arms, gazing down
as if intently making out characters
from a live language he was still learning,
not a smile cracking his pink cheeks.
Gazing down

at the human traffic, of all nations,
the just and the unjust, who
were they, where were they going,
that fine public flow at the edge of which
he waited, poised, detached in wonder
and in no hurry
before he got ready one day
to climb down into its live current.

Night Taxi

for Rod Taylor,
wherever he is

Open city
uncluttered as a map.
I drive through empty streets
scoured by the winds
of midnight. My shift
is only beginning and I am fresh
and excitable, master of the taxi.
I relish my alert reflexes
where all else
is in hiding. I have
by default it seems
conquered me a city.

My first address: I
press the doorbell, I lean back
against the hood, my headlights
scalding a garage door, my engine
drumming in the driveway,
the only sound on the block.
There the fare finds me
like a date, jaunty,
shoes shined, I am
proud of myself, on my toes,
obliging but not subservient.

I take short cuts, picking up
speed, from time to time
I switch on the dispatcher's
litany of addresses,
China Basin to Twin Peaks,
Harrison Street to the Ocean.

I am thinking tonight
my fares are like affairs
—no, more like tricks to turn:
quick, lively, ending up
with a cash payment.
I do not anticipate a holdup.
I can make friendly small talk.
I do not go on about Niggers,
women drivers or the Chinese.
It's all on my terms but
I let them think it's on theirs.

Do I pass through the city
or does it pass through me?
I know I have to be loose,
like my light embrace of the wheel,
loose but in control
—though hour by hour I tighten
minutely in the routine,
smoking my palate to ash,
till the last hour of all
will be drudgery, nothing else.

I zip down Masonic Avenue,
the taxi sings beneath the streetlights
a song to the bare city, it is
my instrument, I woo with it,
bridegroom and conqueror.

I jump out to open the door,
fixing the cap on my head
to, you know, firm up my role,
and on my knuckle
feel a sprinkle of wet.

Glancing upward I see
high above the lamppost
but touched by its farthest light
a curtain of rain already blowing
against black eucalyptus tops.

Acknowledgements

Grateful acknowledgements are made to the editors and publishers of the following publications, in which the poems in this book have appeared:

American Poetry Review, Canto, Christopher Street, Conjunctions, Gay News, Gramercy Review, Inquiry, Listener, London Magazine, Michigan Quarterly Review, New Poetry, New Republic, New York Review of Books, Occident, Paris Review, PN Review, Poetry Book Society Christmas Supplement, Screever, Southern Review, Straight Lines, Threepenny Review, Words Etcetera.

Some first appeared in *Games of Chance*, a limited edition from the Abattoir Press, Nebraska. 'Bally *Power Play*' first appeared as a broadside from Open Door, Toronto. 'The Menace' appeared in *Credences* and as a limited edition published by Manroot. 'Talbot Road' appeared in the *London Magazine* and then as a limited edition published by the Helikon Press. 'New York', 'The Cat and the Wind', and 'The Girls Next Door' first appeared in the *New Yorker*.

The title of the third poem is the name of a specific model of pinball machine.

The streets named in 'At an Intersection' and 'Night Taxi' are all in San Francisco.

The quotation in 'The Menace' is taken from Gregory Bateson, *Steps to an Ecology of Mind*, Paladin, 1973; Ballantine, New York, 1975.